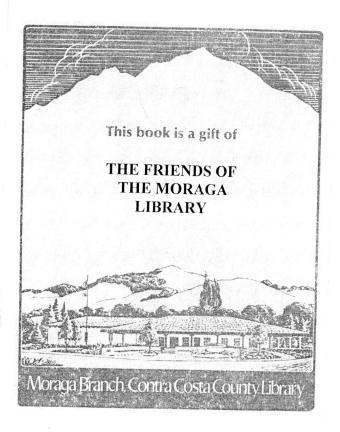

The Pebble First Guide to

Snakes

by Katy R. Kudela

Consulting Editor: Gail Saunders-Smith, PhD

Consultant: Terry Phillip, Curator of Reptiles
Black Hills Reptile Gardens
Rapid City, South Dakota

Capstone
press

Pebble Books are published by Capstone Press,
151 Good Counsel Drive, P.O. Box 669, Mankato, Minnesota 56002.
www.capstonepress.com

1 2 3 4 5 6 14 13 12 11 10 09

Library of Congress Cataloging-in-Publication Data
Kudela, Katy R.
    The pebble first guide to snakes / by Katy R. Kudela.
    p. cm. — (Pebble books. Pebble first guides)
    Summary: "A basic field guide introduces 13 groups of snakes. Includes color
photographs and range maps" — Provided by publisher.
    ISBN-13: 978-1-4296-2243-1 (hardcover)   ISBN-10: 1-4296-2243-1 (hardcover)
    ISBN-13: 978-1-4296-3441-0 (paperback)   ISBN-10: 1-4296-3441-3 (paperback)
    1. Snakes — Juvenile literature. I. Title. II. Series.
QL666.O6K83 2009
597.96 — dc22   2008028235

About Snakes

Scientists have identified at least 3,000 species of snakes, with many subspecies. The snakes featured in this book are grouped into two sections. Venomous snakes are snakes that produce a poison called venom. Nonvenomous snakes do not produce venom.

Note to Parents and Teachers

The Pebble First Guides set supports science standards related to life science. In a reference format, this book describes and illustrates 13 groups of snakes. This book introduces early readers to subject-specific vocabulary words, which are defined in the Glossary section. Early readers may need assistance to read some words and to use the Table of Contents, Glossary, Read More, Internet Sites, and Index sections of the book.

Table of Contents

Cobras

spectacled cobra

Length:	2 to 18 feet (.6 to 5.5 meters)
Eats:	frogs, birds, rodents, snakes, lizards
Lives:	deserts, rain forests, swamps, grasslands
Facts:	• can flatten neck
	• some shoot venom from fangs
	• 23 species

Cobra Range

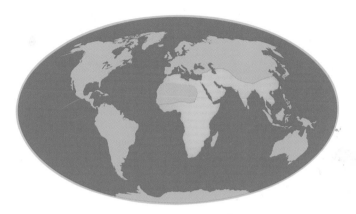

☐ Africa, southern Asia

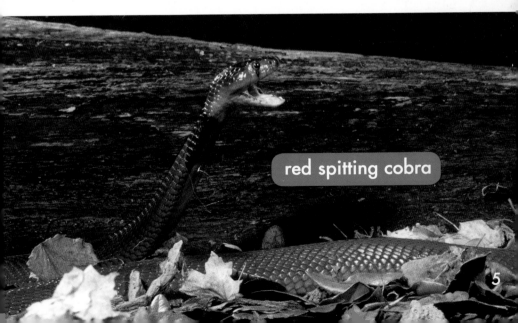

red spitting cobra

Copperheads

broad-banded copperhead

Length:	3 to 4.5 feet (1 to 1.4 meters)
Eats:	frogs, birds, mice, insects
Lives:	woodlands
Facts:	• named for its reddish-brown head
	• moves its tail over leaves to sound like a rattlesnake
	• 5 species

Copperhead Range

☐ eastern North America

southern copperhead

Coral Snakes

eastern coral snake

Length: 1.5 to 4 feet (.5 to 1.2 meters)

Eats: lizards, frogs, snakes

Lives: deserts, grasslands, woodlands, rain forests

Facts:
- bright stripes warn enemies to stay away
- coils body and raises tail to keep head safe from attack
- 69 species

Coral Snake Range

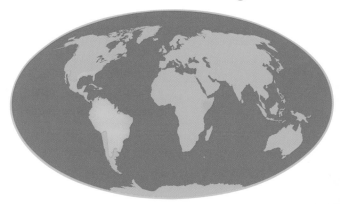

☐ North America, Central America, South America

redtail coral snake

Cottonmouth

Length: 2.5 to 6 feet (.8 to 1.8 meters)

Eats: fish, frogs, snakes, birds, turtles, alligators

Lives: swamps, marshes

Facts:
- opens mouth wide to scare enemies
- also called water moccasin
- 1 species

Cottonmouth Range

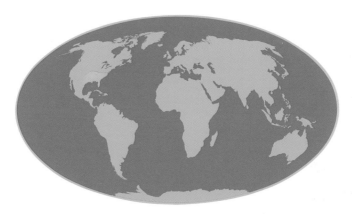

☐ southeastern North America

Mambas

black mamba

Length:	6 to 14 feet (1.8 to 4.3 meters)
Eats:	rodents, birds, lizards
Lives:	forests, grasslands
Facts:	• large eyes see well to find prey
	• black mamba is one of the world's fastest snakes
	• 4 species

Mamba Range

☐ central and southern Africa

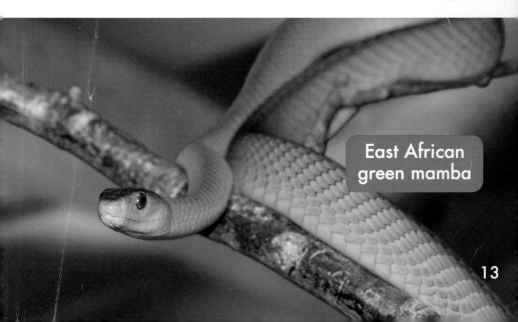

East African
green mamba

13

Puff Adder

Length: 3 to 6 feet (1 to 1.8 meters)

Eats: rodents, birds, lizards

Lives: grasslands

Facts:
- puffs up body to look larger
- fangs are up to 1 inch (2.5 centimeters) long
- 1 species

Puff Adder Range

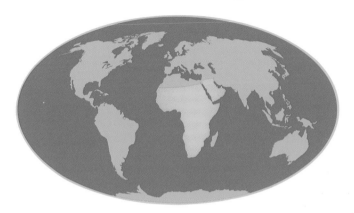

☐ Africa, western Asia

Rattlesnakes

western diamondback rattlesnake

Length: 1 to 8 feet (.3 to 2.4 meters)

Eats: rats, mice, lizards, birds

Lives: grasslands, deserts, forests

Facts:
- shakes rattle on tail to warn enemies
- some hibernate in winter
- 30 species

Rattlesnake Range

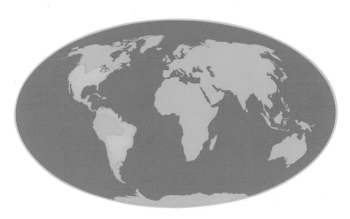

☐ North America, Central America, South America

Southern Pacific
rattlesnake

17

Boa Constrictor

Length:	6 to 18 feet (1.8 to 5.5 meters)
Eats:	birds, lizards, rats, bats, caimans
Lives:	rain forests, grasslands
Facts:	• squeezes prey to death
	• gives birth to live young
	• 1 species

Boa Constrictor Range

☐ Mexico, Central America, South America, Caribbean islands

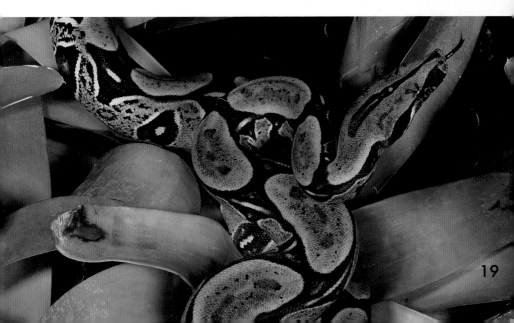

Bull Snake

Length:	5 to 7 feet (1.5 to 2 meters)
Eats:	rodents, birds
Lives:	deserts, forests, grasslands
Facts:	• makes hissing sound when angry
	• one of the largest snakes in North America
	• 1 species

Bull Snake Range

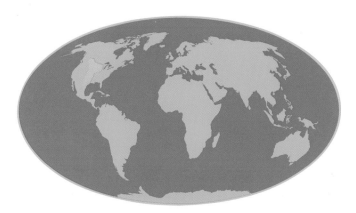

☐ central North America

Garter Snakes

eastern garter snake

Length: 2 to 3 feet (.6 to 1 meter)

Eats: earthworms, fish, frogs, salamanders

Lives: marshes, fields, woodlands

Facts:
- most common snake in North America
- sometimes kept as a pet
- 31 species

Garter Snake Range

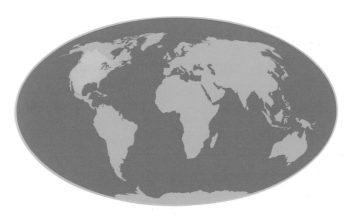

□ North America

blue-striped
garter snake

King Snakes

mountain king snake

Length:	3 to 5 feet (1 to 1.5 meters)
Eats:	rodents, birds, snakes
Lives:	deserts, woodlands, grasslands, forests
Facts:	• some look like the coral snake
	• eats some venomous snakes
	• 9 species

King Snake Range

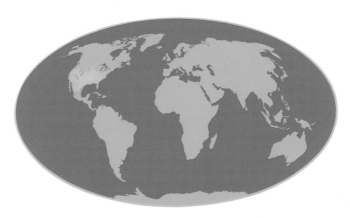

☐ North America

common king snake

Pythons

Indian python

Length: 2 to 30 feet (.6 to 9 meters)

Eats: lizards, birds, fish, frogs, rodents, wild pigs, deer

Lives: rain forests, grasslands, woodlands, swamps, deserts

Facts:
- female coils around her eggs to keep them warm
- good swimmers
- 34 species

Python Range

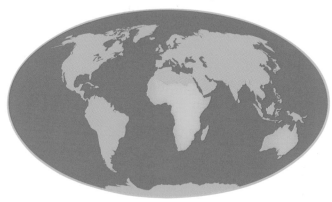

□ Africa, southern Asia, Australia

green tree python

Rat Snakes

black rat snake

Length:	up to 7 feet (2 meters)
Eats:	rodents, birds, bird eggs, frogs, lizards
Lives:	woodlands, forests, swamps
Facts:	• climbs trees to eat birds and eggs • tail gives off stinky musk • 12 species

Rat Snake Range

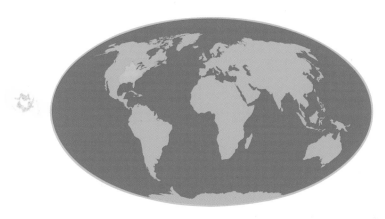

▢ eastern North America

red rat snake

Glossary

coil — to wind or wrap around something

desert — a very dry area of land

fang — a long, hollow tooth; a poison called venom flows through snake fangs.

hibernate — to spend winter in a deep sleep

musk — an oil that some snakes produce when they sense danger

prey — an animal hunted by another animal for food

rodent — a mammal with long front teeth used for gnawing; rats, mice, and squirrels are rodents.

species — a group of animals with similar features; members of a species can mate and produce young.

venomous — having or producing a poison called venom

woodland — land that is covered by trees and shrubs

Read More

Bredeson, Carmen. *Fun Facts about Snakes!* I Like Reptiles and Amphibians! Berkeley Heights, N.J.: Enslow Elementary, 2008.

Lock, Fiona. *Snakes Slither and Hiss*. DK Readers. New York: DK Publishing, 2008.

Internet Sites

FactHound offers a safe, fun way to find educator-approved Internet sites related to this book.

Here's what you do:

1. Visit *www.facthound.com*

2. Choose your grade level.

3. Begin your search.

This book's ID number is 9781429622431.

FactHound will fetch the best sites for you!

Index

Grade: 1
Early-Intervention Level: 22

Editorial Credits
Alison Thiele, set designer; Biner Design, book designer; Jo Miller, photo researcher

Photo Credits
Alamy/blickwinkel/Hecker, 26; David Davis Photoproductions, 28
Bruce Coleman Inc./Joe McDonald, 5, 20; Lynn M. Stone, 10; Maik Dobiey, 12
Getty Images Inc./Minden Pictures/Michael & Patricia Fogden, 9;
   Stone/Phil Schermeister, 21
iStockphoto/Chromix, 4; Mark Kostich, 7; Sergei Chumakov, 27; Sonya Greer,
   cover (rattlesnake)
James P. Rowan, 6
Pete Carmichael, 8, 11, 14, 15, 19, 29
Shutterstock/Amee Cross, 16; Dr. Morley Read, 18; John Bell, 17; Leighton
   Photography & Imaging, 23; Lucian Coman, cover (cobra); nra, 13; Ra'id Khalil, 22;
   Rusty Dodson, 24; Ryan M. Bolton, cover (garter snake); Snowleopard1, cover
   (green mamba)
SuperStock Inc./age fotostock, 25